D0528397

The Best of Bears

The Best of Bears

Photographs by Martin Leman
Words by Jill Leman

PELHAM BOOKS

Old bears,
young bears,

*Baggy bears
and tight ones.*

Big bears, little bears,

———————————————————

Shady bears
and light ones.

Fat bears, thin bears,

———————————

Nosy bears,
polite ones.

Funny bears,
sad bears,

Morning bears
and night ones.

Clever bears,
silly bears,

*Dull bears
and bright ones.*

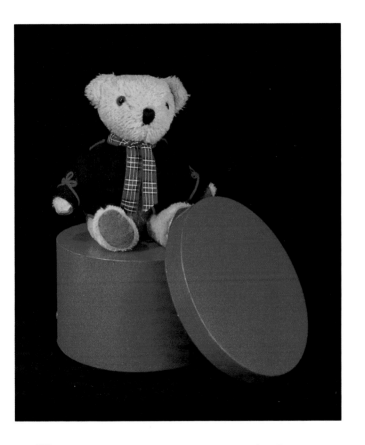

Rough bears, smooth bears,

Eccentric bears
and trite ones.

Every bear's a best bear,

No wrong 'uns
only right 'uns.

Special thanks to the following who
lent their bears to be photographed:
Elizabeth Winthrop, Natalie Gibson,
Hugh Stoneman, Maggie Pringle,
Henrietta, Tom and Daisy Garside,
Deborah Ashforth, Cheryl Wells,
Caroline Duthy, Jackie Wedgwood,
Simon, Jane and Helen Cahill,
Becky and Joshua Viney,
Julia Dummett, Louise Foreman,
Muriel Kenny, Colin Anson,
Harriet Hutton, Paul Dacre.

PELHAM BOOKS

Published by the Penguin Group
27 Wrights Lane, London W8 5TZ
Viking Penguin Inc., 375 Hudson Street, New York, New York 10014, USA
Penguin Books Australia Ltd, Ringwood, Victoria, Australia
Penguin Books Canada Ltd, 10 Alcorn Avenue, Toronto, Ontario, Canada M4V 3B2
Penguin Books (NZ) Ltd, 182-190 Wairau Road, Auckland 10, New Zealand

Penguin Books Ltd, Registered Offices: Harmondsworth, Middlesex, England

First published in Great Britain 1994
Copyright © Martin Leman 1994

Printed and bound in Italy by L.E.G.O

A CIP catalogue record for this book is available from the British Library

ISBN 0 7207 2046 X

The moral right of the author has been asserted